Bath is regarded as one of the loveliest cities in the world. At its heart lies the source of its name and fame – the mysterious hot mineral water springs. The surrounding historical, cultural and architectural heritage has been left by those who came to wonder, worship, swallow or wallow in its waters.

Bath's unique mix of natural and man-made wonders have made it a top tourist attraction in Britain today. It has been welcoming visitors for 2,000 years, from the Romans who built their spectacular spa here, to the stylish 18th century Georgians who gave the city its fashionable elegance and ambience.

This pictorial guide spotlights and explains the city's finest features, vistas and views as they are best seen and enjoyed – on foot during a 90 minute walk.

Bath zählt zu den schönsten Städten der Welt.
Seit 2 000 Jahren werden Besucher in Bath willkommen geheißen, ángefangen von den Römern, die hier einen eindrucksvollen Kurort errichteten, bis zu den feinen Einwohern des 18. Jahrhunderts, die der Stadt ihre modische Eleganz und Atmosphäre verliehen.

Dieser illustrierte Führer macht auf die Besonderheiten der Stadt aufmerksam und weist darauf hin, wie die schönen Ansichten am besten zur Geltung kommen und genossen werden sollten – zu Fuß während weines 1½ stündigen Spaziergangs.

La ville de Bath est reconnue comme étant une des plus belles du monde.
Elle accueille des visiteurs depuis 2000 ans, à partir des Romains qui y ont construit leur impressionnante ville d'eau, jusqu'aux Georgiens du 18ième siècle, qui ont donné à la ville son élégance et ambiance mondaines.

Ce guide illustre met en valeur les plus belles curiosités et les plus beaux panoramas de la ville nieux appreciés durant une excursion à pied d'une heure et demie.

The route then returns to the Roman era, to the museum's collection of artefacts, mosaic flooring and remains excavated from the 18th century to the present day. The leading exhibit is the stone head of Sul (the Gorgon's Head) which adorned the outside of the temple and glared down at anyone entering the temple precinct. (photograph page 3).

Museum cases contain a tin mask (photograph page 4) and the offerings thrown into the sacred spring for good luck. These include silver, bronze and pewter cups, plates, dishes and an oil lamp; carved gemstones and earring, coins (photograph page 3)

The Pump Room and Roman Baths Museum together form the font and focus of Bath.

Water was bubbling from the ground at this spot when Iron Age Celts hailed the spring sacred and worshipped the god Sul there.

Legends of the healing powers of the water stretch back over 2,000 years to the tale of Prince Bladud, a leper who was banished from the court of his father King Lud. Forced to work as a swineherd, he noticed that any pig with a skin disease who wallowed in the warm muddy spring waters was cured. He followed their example, became healed and was accepted back at his father's court. When he in turn became king, he is said to have shown his gratitude by building a bath around the healing spring, lending his name to the city from which Bath is derived.

After invading Britain in AD43, the Romans made a detour from their major route across the country – the great Fosseway road from Exeter to Lincoln – to investigate the steaming swampy spot in the Avon valley so revered by the locals.

With Roman efficiency and engineering ingenuity, in the space of 30-40 years they had drained the marsh, contained the water in a reservoir and built a temple and Britain's first health hydro for restorative and pleasurable purposes. They called their city Aquae Sulis (Sul's Waters) and dedicated their temple to Sulis Minerva, their own goddess of healing.

The entrance in Stall Street to the Pump Room and Roman Baths Museum leads to the King's Lounge which overlooks the King's Bath, built in the 12th century over the original Roman reservoir and principal spring.

The visitor's route then takes a time warp trip into the 18th century Pump Room (photograph page 2). To this elegant Corinthian-columned room fashionable society made their regular visits to drink the waters. Three glasses in the morning were recommended by physicians, although doctors today are sceptical of its powers to ease skin diseases or rheumatic and arthritic conditions.

Sample some from the Pump Room fountain under the cold gaze of the statue of Richard 'Beau' Nash, the man who set the social, dress and etiquette standard for Georgian Bath. Features of the Pump Room include two sedan chairs used to ferry the fashionable around Bath in the Georgian period.

and a selection of lead curses.

The treasured exhibit is the lifesized gilded bronze head of the goddess Minerva (photograph page 5) which would have stood inside the temple. It was found in 1727 by workmen digging a sewer along Stall Street where the temple still lies buried.

Upon the sacrificial altar in front of the temple, offerings to the gods were placed and the entrails of animals examined to foretell the future.

But not all visitors were cured by the mineral waters. Monuments to the dead and stone coffins have been unearthed. While the monuments and altars would have been housed in the temple precinct, the coffins were placed outside the walls of the city.

Other important stone finds include wall panels depicting the Four Seasons, a pediment featuring the Goddess Luna, the head of a Flavian lady with frizzed and coiled hair, and a mask of tragedy which could have come from a tomb, or could possibly indicate the existence of an amphitheatre still hidden under modern Bath.

On the right on leaving the museum can be seen the overflow of the reservoir *(photograph page 6)* which tumbles through the Roman arch on a trilith of stones. Water at the rate of a quarter of a million gallons a day at a temperature of 117 degrees F, 46.5 C wells up from the ground. Each droplet in the torrent today started off as a raindrop that fell ten thousand or

more years ago on the nearby Mendip Hills. It has been on a fantastic journey, trickling through the rock, surging along huge underground gorges and rivers before being forced up from a depth of 2½ - 3 miles from the earth's hot core to emerge here. They are the hottest springs in Britain.

The control of the water supply and drainage displays considerable Roman engineering skills. The original drain and culvert which can be seen carries the constant running spring water to the river some quarter of a mile away.

When the Romans left Britain in AD410 the natives lacked the necessary expertise to cope with the problems of silting and flooding. The site rapidly returned to what it was four centuries before – a marsh – and masonry sunk and collapsed into it.

Sie befinden sich hier am Geburtsort und im Zentrum von Bath. Wasser sprudelte hier schon aus dem Boden, als die Kelten der Eiszeit die dampfende Quelle heilighielten und den Gott Sul anbeteten. Legenden über die Heilkraft des Wassers gehen bis zum Prinzen Bladud, Vater des Königs Lear zurück, der von Lepra geheilt wurde. Kurz nach der römischen Invasion Britanniens im Jahre 43 AD entwässerten die Römer den Sumpfboden, leiteten die heiße Quelle in ein Reservoir und bauten einen Tempel sowie Britanniens ersten Kurort. Sie nannten ihre Stadt Aquae Sulis (die Wasser der Sonne) und widmeten ihren Tempel der Sulis Minerva, ihrer eigenen Göttin der Heilung.

Der Eingang zur Trinkhalle (Pump Room) und zum römischen Bäder Museum (Roman Baths Museum) führt zur Königshalle (King's Lounge) von der Sie auf das Königsbad (King's Bath) schauen können, das im 12. Jahrhundert über das ursprüngliche römische Reservoir und deren Quelle gebaut wurde.

Der Besucher wird dann in die aus dem 18. Jahrhundert stammende Trinkhalle geleitet, wo sich damals die feine Gesellschaft einfand, um das Heilwasser zu trinken. Probieren auch Sie das Mineralwasser vom Brunnen der Trinkhalle. Zu den

C'est l'origine et le foyer de la ville de Bath.

L'eau sortant du sol bouillonnait ici quand les Celtes de l'Age de Fer saluaient la source fumante sacrée et adoraient le Dieu Sul.

Des légendes concernant les pouvoirs curatifs des eaux remontent à 500 ans au Prince Bladud, père du Roi Lear, qui fut guéri de la lèpre.

Peu après l'invasion Romaine de la Grande-Bretagne en 43 ap. J.C., les Romains ont asséché les marécages, retenu l'eau de source chaude dans un réservoir et construit un temple et la première ville d'eau de la Grande-Bretagne. Ils ont appelé leur ville Aquae Sulis (les eaux du soleil) et ont dédié leur temple à Sulis Minerva, leur propre déesse de la guérison.

L'entrée à 'La Pump Room' et 'Roman Baths Museum' mène au 'King's Lounge' (ou Salon du Roi) lequel donne sur le 'King's Bath' (ou Bain du Roi) construit au 12ième siècle au-dessus du réservoir Romain originel et de la source principale.

Le parcours à emprunter par les visiteurs mène ensuite à 'La Pump Room' datant du 18ième siècle où le

besonderen Ausstellungsstücken der Trinkhalle gehören die Statue und das Porträt von Richard 'Beau' Nash, der für das Aufstellen der Gesellschafts-, Kleidungs- und Benehmensregeln im Bath des 18. Jahrhunderts verantwortlich war. Auch 2 Sänften, in denen die feinen Leute durch Bath getragen wurden, sind zu sehen (Foto Seite 2).

Im Museum befinden sich vorgeschichtliche Kunstgegenstände, Mosaikfußböden sowie Ausgrabungen vom 18. Jahrhundert bis zum heutigen Tag. Der Steinkopf des Sul (das Gorgonenhaupt), der die Tempelfassade schmückte, wird als wichtiges Ausstellungsstück gehalten.

Bei weiteren Gegenständen handelt es sich um eine Maske aus Zinn und Opfergaben, die in die heilige Quelle geworfen wurden, um Glück zu bringen, wie z.B. Tassen, Teller, Krüge, geschliffene Edelsteine, Münzen sowie zahlreiche Verfluchungstafeln aus Blei. Das Prunkstück der Ausstellung bildet jedoch der lebensgroße vergoldete Bronzekopf der Göttin Minerva. Er wurde 1727 von Arbeitern, die an einer Abwässerrohrleitung arbeiteten, gefunden.

Grabmäler und Steinsärge wurden ans Tageslicht gebracht. Bei den wichtigen Funden aus Stein handelt es sich um den opferaltar, Wandtafeln, die Vier Jahreszeiten darstellen, den Giebel der Göttin Luna, den Kopf einer Dame des römischen Kaisergeschlechts mit gekräuseltem Haar und Stocklocken, und einer Theatermaske, die darauf schließen läßt, daß unter der Stadt wahrscheinlich auch noch ein Amphitheater verborgen liegt.

Wenn Sie das Museum verlassen, sollten Sie sich rechts den Überlauf der heißen Quelle anschauen, der durch einen römischen Bogen strömt (Foto Seite 6). 1 135 000 Liter Wasser mit einer Temperatur von 46,5°C sprudeln täglich aus der Erde.

Die Wasserversorgung und das Entwässerungssystem demonstrieren wie erfinderisch die römischen Ingenieure waren. Der ursprüngliche Abfluß, der überflüssiges Wasser zum 400 m entfernten Fluß Avon leitet, ist auch noch zu sehen. Im Jahre 410 AD verließen die Römer Britannien und bald darauf verwandelte sich der Ort wieder zu dem, was er 400 Jahre vorher gewesen war: ein Sumpf. Das Mauerwerk sank ein, stürzte zusammen und wurde mit dem Schlamm und Schutt der Jahrhunderte bedeckt.

beau monde venait boire les eaux. Goûtez l'eau de la fontaine du 'Pump Room'. Les élèments les plus impressionnants de La 'Pump Room' comprennent une statue et un portrait de Richard 'Beau' Nash, l'homme qui établit les valeurs sociales de tenue et de comportement de la ville de Bath Georgienne. On peut voir deux chaises à porteurs qui transportaient le beau monde dans Bath. (Photo page 2)

Le musée contient les artefacts, les parterres en mosaic et les vestiges découverts depuis le 18iéme siècle à nos jours. La tête en pierre de Sul (Tête de Gorgon) qui décorait la façade du temple est l'un des objets les plus importants. (photo page 3).

Les objets exposés comprennent un masque en fer (photo page 4) et des offrandes que l'on jetait dans la source sacrée pour la bonne chance-tasses, assiettes, plats, pierres précieuses taillées, pièces de monnaie et plusieurs tablettes en plomb gravées de malédictions. La tête en bronze dorée de grandeur nature de la déesse Minerva (photo page 5) est l'objet le plus précieux de l'exposition. Elle fut trouvée en 1727 par des ouvriers qui creusaient un caniveau.

Des monuments aux morts et des cercueils en pierre ont été déterrés. D'autres découvertes importantes en pierre comprennent l'autel à sacrifices, des panneaux aux murs représentant les Quatre Saisons, le fronton de la déesse Luna, la tête d'une dame Flavienne aux cheveux frisés et bouclés, et un masque de tragédie ce qui indiquerait qu'un amphithéâtre se trouverait peut-être toujours enseveli sous la ville moderne de Bath.

En quittant le musée sur la droite se tient le trop-plein de la source chaude bouillonnant sous une voûte Romaine. (photo page 6). Un quart d'un million de litres d'eau par jour à une température de 117 degrés F., 46.5 degrés C., jaillit du sol.

La régularisation des eaux et leur système d'ecoulement montre la grande habileté technique des Romains. On peut voir le caniveau originel emportant l'excédent d'eau vers la rivière Avon 400 mètres plus loin.

Après le départ des Romains de la Grande-Bretagne, cet emplacement redevint très vite ce qu'il était quatre siècles auparavant – un marécage – et la maçonnerie s'y est affaissée puis effondrée pour être en partie recouverte de vase et de décombres des siècles.

most impressive feature of all, the Great Bath *(photograph fold out, backcover page 7)* which you face on leaving the museum.

The Great Bath was discovered by the Victorians who were investigating a leak from the King's Bath in the 1860's. In the space of 20 years, surrounding property was bought, overlying buildings pulled down and the site excavated so that the public could view the bath. When rebuilding they could not resist adding their own embellishments, and all masonry about shoulder level including the statues seen today were added by the Victorians.

The Baths grew from the first century AD into the vast sophisticated complex that existed into the early years of the fifth century. Alterations and improvements made its development a continuous process. Its paying customers enjoyed heated rooms, saunas, a 'whirlpool', Turkish baths, exercise rooms, hot cubicles, treatment rooms, plunge pools and the

The Great Bath, used by the Romans as a warm swimming pool, is a spectacular 80 ft by 40 ft in size and was the centrepiece of the baths complex. It was originally a great hall with windows and barrel-vaulted roof. Hollow box tiles were cemented together for the roof, which discouraged the formation of cold droplets of condensation falling on the bathers below. Each box tile had the mark of the maker, and a sample of this engineering technology – the only remnant of Roman roofing in this country – can be seen in a recess flanking the Great Bath.

Several tons of lead sheeting which came from the flourishing mineworks in the Mendip Hills during the Roman period lines the floor of the Great Bath. Hot water flows directly from the reservoir and a section of the lead conduit can be seen.

Alcoves along the sides of the Great Bath allowed onlookers to sit, gossip, read and relax, buy drink, food or souvenirs away from the splashes of the bathers. There is a diving stone *(photograph page 8)* although the depth of the bath is only 5 ft.

Turning left from the museum into the East Baths is a sunken semi-circular bath set into a wall recess. Bathers immersed themselves to the neck in the curative waters and it is thought that slaves with bellows agitated the waters, making this a forerunner of today's jacuzzi.

Opposite this bath is the warm plunge Lucas Bath, named after Dr. Lucas who discovered it in 1755. The East Baths, which include a series of hypocaust rooms heated by hot air flowing under the floor, were built up on five successive occasions to avoid the continual threat of flooding.

In the West Baths at the opposite end of the Great Bath, bathers stripped in a changing room (apodyterium) moved into the hottest rooms (caldarium) for scraping, oiling, cleaning, and hair and hard skin removal, then moved through to the tepidarium to cool gently before an invigorating cold plunge in the Circular Bath (frigidarium). *(photograph page 9)* An intensely hot area was called a laconicum, favoured by the brave before a cold dip.

The Roman central heating system was sophisticated and efficient. Hot air heated by a furnace outside the rooms was drawn by ducted flue through the rooms and under the flooring which was raised on piles. Hollow box tiles were used to build hot 'igloos' and to ensure even underfloor heat. *(photograph page 9).*

The Roman windows to the right of the Circular Bath offer a view of the King's Bath *(photograph page 8).* Through the arch, Romans threw their offerings to the gods as this is the site of the sacred spring and reservoir, now overlaid by the King's Bath. Statues placed in the water by the Romans gave a stagey and spectacular vision shimmering through the rising steam of people walking on water.

Although most of the Roman Baths stayed hidden for centuries, the principal hot spring still gushed and monks ran what remained as a healing centre. Throughout its obscure days, visitors still came to drink and bathe. Five mediaeval baths were in use in the 16th century, but they were sleasy, squalid and disreputable. A visit in the early 1600's from Anne, wife of James I seeking a cure for dropsy followed by a selection of visiting royals heralded the start of Bath's revival and respectability to its Georgian heyday.

Die Bäder wurden vom 1. Jahrhundert AD bis zum Beginn des 5. Jahrhunderts AD zu einer bewundernswerten Badeanstalt entwickelt, die Besucher von ganz Europa sowie auch Britannien anzog. Die Kurgäste genossen schon damals geheizte Räume, Saunen, ein Kneippbecken, türkische Dampfbäder, Turnhallen, heiße Bäder, Behandlungsräume, kalte Bäder und vor allem das eindrucksvolle große Schwimmbecken (Great Bath), das vor Ihnen liegt, wenn Sie das Museum verlassen. (Foto Seite 7)

Nach der Entdeckung des großen Schwimmbeckens in den sechziger Jahren des 19. Jahrhunderts vergingen 20 Jahre, bis alle in der Nähe befindlichen Grundstücke gekauft werden konnten, die Gebäude, die sich über dem Bad befanden beseitigt und es schließlich ausgegraben

Lukastauchbad (Lucas Bath), befinden. Die Fußöden in den Ostbädern mußten fünf mal hintereinander auf ein höheres Niveau angehoben werden, um Überschwemmungen zu vermeiden.

Auf der gegenüberliegenden Seite des großen Schimmbeckens befinden sich die Westbäder (West Baths), in denen mehrere Behandlungsräume verschiedener Wärmegrade untergebracht waren, die durch ein fortschrittliches System, das warme Luft durch Rohre zirkulierte, wirksam beheizt werden konnten.

Durch die Fenster, die das Königsbad (King's Bath) überblicken, warfen die Römer ihre Opfergaben zu Ehren der Götter, da sich damals an dieser Stelle die heilige Quelle und das Reservoir befanden.

Nachdem die Römer Britannien verlassen hatten, benutzten Mönche was von der Anlage übriggeblieben

que vous pouvez voir en face de vous dès que vous quittez le musée. (photo page 7).

Depuis sa découverte en 1860, il a fallu 20 ans pour acheter le territoire d'alentour, démolir les bâtiments qui le recouvraient et excaver le terrain, avant d'être enfin ouvert au public. Toute la maçonnerie au-dessus de nos têtes, ainsi que les statues, ont été ajoutées à cette époque.

Le 'Great Bath', une piscine chaude mesurant 24 mètres par 12 mètres, était autrefois couverte. Vous pouvez voir une partie de la toiture recouverte de tuiles dans un recoin à côté du 'Great Bath'.

Plusieurs tonnes de feuilles de plomb tapissent le fond du 'Great Bath'. L'eau chaude coule directement du réservoir.

En tournant à gauche à la sortie du musée, vous trouverez les Thermes Est qui comprennent une série d'hypocaustes, un bain profond à 'tourbillon d'eau', bas et semi-circulaire et le bain (pour plonger) chaud 'Lucas'. Les parterres des Thermes est ont été levés cinq fois successivement pour éviter toute menace d'inondation.

Dans les Thermes Ouest du côté opposé au 'Great Bath' existaient plusieurs salles de traitement de différentes températures chauffées efficacement par un système sophistiqué de conduites d'air chaud.

werden konnte und somit der Öffentlichkeit zugänglich gemacht wurde.

Das Mauerwerk über Schulterhöhe einschließblich der Statuen wurde zu jener Zeit hinzugefügt.

Das große Schwimmbecken ist 24 m lang und 12 m breit, wurde als warmes Bad benutzt und war ursprünglich überdacht. Ein Beispiel des Daches, aus Backstein gefertigt, befindet sich in einer seitlichen Nische.

Der Boden des großen Schwimmbeckens ist mit Bleiplatten ausgelegt, die mehrere Tonnen wiegen. Heißes Wasser wird direkt vom Reservoir zugeführt.

Wenn Sie das Museum verlassen und sich nach links wenden, gelangen Sie zu den Ostbädern (East Baths), wo sich mehrere Hypocaust-Räume, ein versenktes halbkreisförmiges Kneippbecken sowie das warme

war als Heilzentrum. Sogar während der für die Stadt relativ unbedeutenden Jahre, die folgten, kamen Kurgäste, einschließlich der königlichen Familie, nach Bath, um das Wasser zu trinken und um zu baden.

A partir du premier siècle ap.J.C. jusqu'au 5ième siècle, les Thermes se développèrent en un centre sophistiqué attirant des visiteurs d'Europe aussi bien que de Grande-Bretagne. Ses clients profitèrent des pièces chauffées, des saunas, d'un 'tourbillon d'eau'; des bains turcs, des gymnases, des cabines chaudes, des bains pour plonger, et du 'Great Bath' (ou Grand Bain), le plus impressionnant monument de tous,

Les Romains jetaient leurs offrandes aux Dieux par les fenêtres donnant sur le 'King's Bath', (photo page 8) car c'est ici qu'étaient le ruisseau sacré et le réservoir.

Après le départ des Romains, des moines firent ce qui restait un centre de guérison. Même durant les périodes où Bath était moins connue, les visiteurs y compris les membres de la famille royale venaient à Bath pour boire et se baigner dans les eaux.

From the Roman remains, the route now retraces the glorious years of 18th century Georgian Bath, reflected today in its golden stone buildings.

Three men transformed the city – Richard 'Beau' Nash, a gambler; Ralph Allen, an entrepreneur and John Wood, an architect. The first provided the social tone, the second the stone and the third the classic style that set the standard for the developing city.

Bath Street with its graceful colonnades faces you as you leave the Roman Museum. It was built in 1789 to form a covered link between the main Pump Room and Baths to the Cross Bath which is fed by one of the city's three hot springs. In the 17th and 18th centuries, this bath was favoured by people of 'quality and rank'. A Roman reservoir lies beneath it.

Turn right and walk a few steps along Stall Street to a small colonnade to the right which opens out a view of Abbey Churchyard (*photograph page 10*). The north front of the Pump Room, designed by Thomas Baldwin, bears the Greek inscription Water Is Best.

The Abbey's majestic west front faces the Churchyard and a staggered line of eighteenth century buildings, now shops and a cafe complete the square. The National Trust shop was formerly the home of Major George Wade, who financed Ralph Allen in his early business ventures in Bath.

Buskers (*photograph page 11*) are now a regular feature in the Abbey Churchyard, although 300 years ago

Defoe described the area as a centre for raffling, gaming and levity.

Return to Stall Street, turn right and walk to the junction of Cheap Street (from the old English word 'chepe' meaning market). The route up Union Street passes two picturesque shopping avenues on the right: The Corridor, a covered arcade, and Northumberland Place (*page 12*).

At the corner of Union Street and Upper Borough Walls stands the

Royal Mineral Water Hospital, built by John Wood, using stone supplied by Ralph Allen financed by money collected from the visitors by Richard Nash and supported by Bath's leading physician, Dr. William Oliver who invented the Bath Oliver biscuit as an antidote to rich food. A guide to how patients fared after treatment there in the years 1742-1769 lists:-
Cured 1,853; Much Better 2,773; Incurable 355; Improper 773; Irregular 78; Dead 169.

The hospital's £3 admission fee either paid the patient's fare home or for their burial.

Die folgende Route durch Bath läßt die glorreichen Jahre des 18. Jahrhunderts wieder aufleben, die auch heute noch in den goldenen Steingebäuden reflektiert werden.

Drei Persönlichkeiten waren für die Verwandlung der Stadt hauptsächlich verantwortlich: Richard 'Beau' Nash, der das Gesellschaftsleben organisierte, Ralph Allen, ein Geschäftsmann, dessen Steinbruch den Sandstein für die Gebäude lieferte und John Wood, ein Architekt.

Wenn Sie das römische Museum verlassen, sehen Sie gegenüber die eleganten Kolonnaden der Bath Street. Sie wurde 1789 gebaut und bildet eine überdachte Verbindung zwischen der Trinkhalle (Pump Room) und einem weiteren Bad, Kreuzbad (Cross Bath) genannt, unter dem sich die zweite Heilquelle der Stadt befindet.

Wenn Sie der Stall Street nach rechts folgen und dann durch die kleine Kolonnade auf der rechten Seite gehen, befinden Sie sich auf dem Abbey Churchyard, wo Straßenmusikanten regelmäßig zu finden sind (Foto Seite 10/11). Die griechische Inschrift an der Nordseite der Trinkhalle bedeutet: "Wasser ist am bestern". Die Westseite der' Abbey' und Gebäude aus dem 18. Jahrhundert, in denen sich hauptsächlich Geschäfte.

Kehren Sie zur Stall Street zurück und gehen Sie rechts bix zur Kreuzung weiter. Überqueren Sie Cheap Street und führen Sie Ihren Spaziergang in der Union Street fort, von der, auf der rechten Seite, 2 hübsche Gassen mit interessanten Geschäften 'The Corridor' und Northumberland Place, abgegen. (Foto Seite 12)

An der Ecke Union Street/Upper Borough Walls befindet sich das königliche Mineralwasserkrankenhaus (Royal Mineral Water Hospital), das hauptsächlich von Beau Nash, der alle wohlhabenden Besucher um Spenden bat, finanziert wurde. Außerdem wurde es von dem damals führenden Arzt in Bath, William Oliver, unterstützt, der den Bath Oliver Biskuit, als Verdauungsmittel für reichhaltige Speisen, erfunden hatte.

Le parcours retrace maintenant les années glorieuses de la ville Georgienne de Bath du 18ième siècle, se reflétant aujourd'hui dans ses bâtiments en pierre dorée.

Trois hommes transformèrent cette ville, Richard 'Beau' Nash qui organisa la vie sociale de Bath; Ralph Allen, homme d'affaires dont la carrière a fourni la pierre de Bath pour la construction, et John Wood, architecte.

Les élégantes colonnades de 'Bath Street' se situent en face de vous lorsque vous quittez le musée Romain. Bâti en 1789, elles forment une liaison abritée entre la 'Pump Room' principle et un autre bain – 'Cross Bath' – qui est nourri par une des trois sources de la ville.

Tournez à droite, 'Stall Street' s'étend en une petite colonnade sur la droite. Vous vous trouvez à 'Abbey Churchyard' où l'on voit souvent des artistes jouer. (photo page 10/11) Sur la façade nord de La 'Pump Room' on peut lire l'inscription en Grec: 'l'eau est ce qu'il y a de meilleur'. La façade Ouest de l'abbaye donne sur la place de l'église et plusieurs bâtiments du 18ième siècle, maintenant occupés par des magasins complètent la place.

Retournez a 'Stall Street', tournez à droite et marchez jusqu 'au

croisement de 'Cheap Street'. Traverse
vers 'Union Street' et vous passerez
devant deux avenues pittoresques de
magasins sur la droite, le 'Corridor' et
'Northumberland Place'.
(photo page 12)
  Au coin de 'Union Street' et de
'Upper Borough Walls' se tient le
'Royal Mineral Water Hospital', lequel
fut financé avec l'argent recueilli des
visiteurs par Richard Nash et secondé
par le premier docteur
Georgien de Bath, William Oliver, qui
inventa les biscuits 'Bath Oliver'
comme antidote contre la nourriture
riche.

Turn left into Upper Borough Walls, which includes part of a restored mediaeval wall resting on an original Roman wall, then right into Queen Street. This area is early Georgian with cobbled roads and bow windows. Trim Street, which crosses Queen Street, features an arch across the road which is called Trim Bridge *(photograph page 13)* General Wolfe, hero of the Battle of Quebec (1759) lived at number 5.

Continue along Queen Street then turn left into Wood Street to face Queen Square *(photograph page 14).* Begun in 1729, this was the first major project of John Wood, two years after he arrived in Bath from London with a flair for what was fashionable. Queen Square, named after Queen Caroline, wife of George II, was Wood's interpretation of the Palladian architectural style. Planned to resemble a palace with forecourt, the north side has the grandest facade with bays and Corinthian columns. John Wood himself lived in the square he designed. Dr. William Oliver was another famous resident. Number 13 is just one of the houses occupied by author Jane Austen in Bath on her visits.

The obelisk in the centre commemorates the visit of Frederick, Prince of Wales.

The bow-fronted merchant's house (now an insurance office) at the corner of Gay Street and Old King Street off Queen Square features a small powder room to the right of the front door. Through the window can be seen Delft tiles surrounding the powder bowl, which contained powder for wigs.

Turn left into Queen's Parade, noting on the left the two small pavilions built for waiting sedan chair men to keep them away from the inns and liquor that made them rude and abusive to customers. This attempt at regulation was a forerunner of Hackney Carriage licensing.

Across the road on the right are steps leading to Gravel Walk where the hopeful paraded to catch the eye of the available. Alongside the steps runs Royal Avenue and the entrance to Royal Victoria Park.

A detour along Royal Avenue through the park leads to the Botanical Gardens, an extensive and exquisite collection of plants from all parts of the world.

Biegen Sie nach links in die Upper Borough Walls ein, und dann nach rechts in die Queen Street. Die Straße, die sie kreuzt heißt Trim Street. Sie wird durch den schönen Bogen, der sie überspannt und den man Trim Bridge nennt, interessant. (Foto Seite 13) Gehen Sie durch die Queen Street weiter und biegen Sie dann nach links in die Wood Street ein, die in den Queen Square einmündet. (Foto Seite 14) Die Bauarbeiten für diesen Platz begannen im Jahre 1729. Er wurde so entworfen als stelle er einen Palast mit Vorhof dar und zählte zum ersten großen Projekt des Architekten John Wood, der hier selbst wohnte. Die Schriftstellerin Jane Austin, lebte in Nr. 13.

In dem Haus mit dem Erker an der Ecke Gay Street/Old King Street, am Queen Squsre ist ein kleines Toilettenzimmer rechts neben der Eingangstür sichtbar. Fliesen aus Delft umgeben die Puderschale, die Perückenpuder enthält.

Biegen Sie jetzt nach links in die Queens Parade ein und Sie werden auf der linken Seite zwei kleine Pavillone sehen, die für die auf Aufträge wartenden Sänftenträger gebaut wurden. Überqueren Sie die Straße und biegen Sie in die Royal Avenue ein mit dem Eingang zum königlichen Viktoriapark (Royal Victoria Park). Wenn Sie ganz bis zum Ende der Royal Avenue laufen und dann durch den Park weitergehen, gelangen Sie schließlich zu den Botanischen Gärten, wo Sie eine umfassende Sammlung außergewöhnlicher Pflanzen aus aller Welt vorfinden werden.

Tournez à gauche dans 'Upper Borough Walls', puis à droite dans 'Queen Street'. 'Trim Street' qui la traverse possède une vôute au-dessus de la route appelée 'Trim Bridge'. (photo page 13)

Continuez jusqu'à 'Queen Street' puis tournez à gauche dans 'Wood Street' pour vous trouver dans 'Queen Square'. (photo page 14) Commencé en 1729, ce fut le premier projet de l'architecte John Wood et fut conçu pour ressembler à un palace et son avant-cour. John Wood même y a résidé. L'auteur Jane Austen a vécu au no. 13.

La maison marchande à façade bombée située au coin de 'Gay Street' et 'Old King Street' près de 'Queen Square' possède une toilette à droite de la porte d'entrée. La cuvette qui contenait de la poudre pour perruques est entourée de carreaux en faience de Delft.

Tournez à gauche dans 'Queen's Parade' et vous remarquerez les deux petits pavillons à gauche construits pour ceux qui portaient les 'chaises-à-porteurs'; ils attendaient là. Traversez la rue et allez dans 'Royal Avenue' et à l'entrée du 'Royal Victoria Park'. Un détour le long de 'Royal Avenue' à travers le parc vous amène aux 'Botanical Gardens' qui ont une collection extensive et exquise de plantes venant des quatre coins du monde.

From Royal Avenue, the full splendour of Royal Crescent *(photograph page 15 and centre page)* can be viewed. Built in a 600 ft. sweeping arc, its 30 houses stand behind a flourish of 114 Ionic columns. The Crescent, described as the finest in Europe, epitomises the peak of Palladian style architecture in Bath. Its hilltop position gives an unrivalled view over the city.

Number 1 Royal Crescent is now a museum which recreates an authentic Georgian interior in one of Bath's most fashionable addresses. It is restored to the style enjoyed by its former illustrious residents, who included the Duke of York in 1796 and the Princess de Lamballe, Lady-in-Waiting to Marie Antoinette of France. Number 1 Royal Crescent is pictured.

Sir Isaac Pitman, inventor of the Pitman system of shorthand lived at number 17; Elizabeth Linley eloped from number 11 with statesman and dramatist Sheridan.

The aerial view shows the two architectural masterpieces of Bath designed by father and son. The Circus in the foreground was designed by John Wood the Elder. Royal Crescent was designed by John Wood the Younger, who was also responsible for Brock Street which links the two stately and outstanding landmarks. Walk to the end of Brock Street to the Circus.

Von der Royal Avenue aus, können Sie den Blick auf den prachtvollen 'Royal Crescent' (Foto Seite 15, 16-17) ganz besonders genießen. Es wird als das schönste halbmondförmige Gebäude Europas betrachtet, und die darin enthaltenen 30 Häuser wurden in einem 180m langen weitläufigen Bogen gebaut. 'Royal Crescent' Number 1 dient jetzt als Museum und wurde ganz im Stil des 18. Jahrhunderts eingerichtet.

Die Luftaufnahme zeigt die zwei architektonischen Meisterwerke, die von Vater und Sohn für Bath entworfen wurden (Foto Seite 19). Der im Vordergrund befindliche 'Circus' wurde von John Wood sen. entworfen. John Wood jun. entwarf den 'Royal Crescent' sowie auch Brock Street, die die beiden imposanten und außergewöhnlichen Wahrzeichen verbindet. Laufen Sie durch die Brock Street bis zum 'Circus'.

On peut apprécier toute la splendeur de 'Royal Crescent' depuis 'Royal Avenue'. (photo page 15, 16-17) Considéré comme étant le plus beau croissant d'Europe, ses 30 maisons sont construites en une majestueuse courbe continue de 200 mètres. Le no. 1 de 'Royal Crescent' est aujourd'hui un musée recréant un intérieur authentique Georgien.

La vue aérienne (photo page 19) montre les deux chefs-d'oeuvres architecturaux de Bath conçus par père et fils. Le 'Circus' au premier plan fut conçu par John Wood – père – Royal Crescent fut conçu par John Wood – fils – de même que 'Brock Street' liant les deux points de repère les plus remarquables et majestueux. Marchez ensuite jusqu'au bout de 'Brock Street' vers le 'Circus'.

John Wood the Elder was fired and inspired to recreate the great imperial structures of Rome itself in Bath. The Circus (photograph page 20) is considered his greatest design, although he died in 1754 as work was beginning. His son saw it to completion.

Three curved crescents, form a circle, 318 ft in diameter. The terraces all display a unified front featuring the three classical design forms, Doric, Ionic and Corinthian and a frieze showing symbols of the arts and occupations.

Famous residents included Dr. David Livingstone the missionary and explorer; Lord Clive of India; Thomas Gainsborough the painter and William Pitt, MP and Prime Minister.

The Assembly Rooms in Bennett Street (reached by turning left from the Circus) were the social centre of late Georgian Bath. The fashionable flocked there to dine and dance, gossip and gamble, to flirt and flaunt their finery and to see and be seen. The social pecking order was rigorously observed within its elegant suite of rooms under its Masters of Ceremonies.

The Assembly Rooms were de-signed and built by John Wood the Younger and built between 1769-71. Known as the Upper Rooms, they were considered the finest in Europe and were in continual use from serving 2,000 people from public breakfasts to grand balls. Johann Strauss, Liszt, Rubenstein and Charles Dickens were among the many who performed there.

Now restored after war damage and a lapse into decay and indignity as a cinema and saleroom, the Assembly Rooms comprise a 106 ft long ball-room, (photograph page 21) the largest 18th century room in Bath with chandeliers made by William Parker of Fleet Street, London, the Octagon card room, the Long Card Room and Tea Room. Surrounding the suite of rooms are corridors known as 'corridors of scandal' where ladies retired to cool off and exchange tales and tattle. Visitors could be brought to the doors of the function rooms in sedan chair via the corridors. Tea dances are still held at the Assembly Rooms in spring and autumn.

Doris Langley Moore's world famous Museum of Costume is housed in the Assembly Rooms and features fashions from the late 16th century to the present day.

Admiral Arthur Phillip, first Gov-ernor of New South Wales and Founder of Australia lived at number 19 Bennett Street. A memorial service is held at the Abbey on his birthday, October 11.

On leaving the Assembly Rooms turn left, cross Alfred Street and turn right into Bartlett Street. This is the antique centre of Bath. Continue to the end and cross George Street to approach Milsom Street to the right.

The quality shops that line Milsom Street made it a fashionable place to shop in the 19th century, just as now. The National Centre of Photography on the left was a circulating library and reading rooms where probably Jane Austen enjoyed reading the 'gothic' novels that inspired her Bath-based pastiches.

The paved area at the foot of Milsom Street is Old Bond Street. Take the left turn into New Bond Street and continue to the end to the main Post Office. A detour left here leads to Bath Postal Museum in Broad Street where the world's first postage stamp was posted on May 2 1840. (photograph page 22).

Return to the modern Post Office, turn right and cross the High Street at the Guildhall.

Der 'Circus' (Foto Seite 20) der uns an die großartigen Bauten in Rom erinnern soll, wird als der beste Entwurf von John Wood sen. bezeichnet, obwohl er im Jahre 1754, als die Arbeiten begannen, starb. Sein Sohn hat das Werk jedoch vollendet. 3

halbmondförmige Gebäude bilden einen Kreis mit einem Durchmesser von 95,5 m. Zu den berühmten Bewohnern gehörten Dr. David Livingstone, der Missionar und Forscher, Thomas Gainsborough, der Maler und William Pitt, der später

Premier Minister wurde.
In Bennet Street, die in den Circus einmündet, befinden sich die Versammlungsräume, die für die Gesellschaft im Bath des 18. Jahrhunderts verschiedene wichtige Funktionen erfüllten. Von John Wood entworfen und zwischen 1769-71 erbaut, waren sie in ständigem Gebrauch, vom Frühstück für 2 000 Personen angefangen bis zu den großen Gesellschaftsbällen am Abend. Johann Strauss, Liszt, Rubenstein und Charles Dickens u.v.a. traten hier auf. Die frühere Pracht der Räume wurde wieder hergestellt und man kann den Ballsaal mit seinen herrlichen Kronleuchtern (Foto Seite 21), das achteckige Kartenspielzimmer (Octagon Card Room), das lange Kartenspielzimmer (Long Card Room) und das Teezimmer (Tea Room) besichtigen. Korridore, die von den Sänftenträgern benutzt wurden, um ihre Kunden bis zu den Zimmertüren

zu tragen, umranden alle Räume. Auch das Kostümmuseum der Doris Langley Moore wurde in den Versammlungsräumen untergebracht und enthält Kleidungsartikel von 400 Jahren.

Wenn Sie die Versammlungsräume verlassen, gehen Sie nach links weiter, überqueren Alfred Street und biegen dann rechts in die Bartlett Street, dem Antiquitätenzentrum von Bath, ein. Laufen Sie bis zum Ende dieser Straße und überqueren Sie George Street und vor Ihnen rechts liegt dann die Milsom Street, in der sich viele gute Geschäfte befinden. Am Ende dieser Straße biegen Sie links in die New Bond Street ein und laufen bis zur nächsten Ecke, wo sich das Hauptpostamt befindet. (Ein kleiner Umweg nach links führt zum Post Museum von Bath (Bath Postal Museum) in der Broad Street, wo die erste Briefmarke der Welt am 2. Mai 1840 aufgegeben wurde) (Foto Seite 22).

Biegen Sie nach rechts ab und überqueren Sie die High Street vor dem Rathaus (Guildhall).

Le 'Circus' (ou cirque), rappelant les grands édifices impériaux de Rome même, fut considéré comme étant le plus beau projet de John Wood – père – quoiqu'il mourut en 1754 alors que les travaux commençaient. (photo page 20) Son fils s'assura de l'achèvement des travaux. Trois croissants forment un cercle de près de 100 mètres de diamètre. D'importantes personnalités y résidaient dont Dr David Livingstone, missionnaire et explorateur, Thomas Gainsborough, peintre et William Pitt, qui devint Premier Ministre.

Dans 'Bennett Street' près du 'Circus' vous trouverez les 'Assembly Rooms' qui étaient le centre social de la ville Georgienne de Bath. Conçues par John Wood – fils – et construites entre 1769 et 1771, elles furent trés fréquentées, servant jusqu'a 2000 personnes pour le petite-déjeuner et les grands bals du soir. Johann Stauss, Liszt, Rubenstein et Charles Dickens jouerent ici. Les Pièces ont été restorées et ont retrouvé leur ancien éclat; elles comprennent une salle de bal avec de magnifiques lustres, (photo page 21) la salle 'Octagon Card Room', la 'Long Card Room' et Salon de Thé. Les couloirs qui étaient utilisés par les porteurs de chaises qui déposaient les clients aux portes, entourent les salles. Le 'Doris Langley Moore's Museum of Costume' se trouve dans les 'Assembly Rooms' et montre la mode de quatre siècles.

Lorsque vous sortez des 'Assembly Rooms', tournez à gauche, traversez 'Alfred Street' et tournez à nouveau à

droite dans 'Bartlett Street', centre des antiquaires de Bath. Continuez jusqu'au bout de la rue et traversez 'George Street' pour arrivers à 'Milsom Street' sur la droite, la rue des grands magasins. Au bout de la rue, tournez à gauche dans 'New Bond Street' et continuez jusqu'à la Poste Centrale au coin. Un détour vous mène au 'Bath Postal Museum' dans 'Broad Street' où le premier timbre du monde fut posté le 2 mai 1840 (photo page 22).

Retournez à la Poste Centrale, tournez à droite et traversez le 'High Street' près du 'Guildhall'.

While fashionable society of quality and status danced and dined at the Assembly Rooms, wealthy traders of Bath who were kept out sought a rival venue for their own gatherings: the Banqueting Hall in the Guildhall *(photograph page 23)*. It is one of the finest rooms in the Adam style in Europe and is hung with portraits by Reynolds and three exquisite Whitefriars glass chandeliers. It was opened in 1776, originally designed by Thomas Baldwin for use as the town hall.

Next door to the Guildhall is the Market, where browsers can find anything from a fresh fish to an antique silver fork with which to eat it. Local specialties like Bath Chaps (pigs' cheeks) are available here. A market pillar or 'nail' was set in the present market in 1786 and upon it deals were struck. The term 'pay on the nail' refers to cash transactions conducted in this way.

Through the market to Grand Parade, turn left and with the Victoria Art Gallery to the left, cross to Pulteney Bridge on your right.

Pulteney Bridge *(photograph page 25)* was built by Robert Adam in 1771 following a competition among architects. It is the only bridge in England with shops on both sides. Look ahead to Argyle Street and beyond the Laura Place fountain to the most imposing boulevard in Bath: Great Pulteney Street *(photograph page 24)*. Its former residents are a roll-call of the famous and infamous: Louis Napoleon, later Napoleon III; Mrs Maria Fitzherbert who was secretly married to the Prince of Wales, later King George IV; Lady Hamilton, Lord Nelson's mistress; William Wilberforce who abolished slavery, and Thomas Baldwin, Bath city architect who designed Great Pulteney Street.

Crowning the 1,100 ft long street is the Holburne and Menstrie Museum housing an important collection of works of art and a centre for modern crafts.

Return to Pulteney Bridge and go down the steps to the banks of the River Avon to take a riverside stroll. A puppet theatre can be found at the foot of the bridge shops overlooking Pulteney weir.

Across the river is the East Gate, a reminder of Bath's mediaeval roots. Monks who built up the flourishing woollen cloth trade using Cotswold sheep brought the fleeces to the river at this point. Walk on until you are level with the Empire Hotel, a large building whose skyline features a castle, a manorial house and a cottage so that guests could feel at home, whatever their class.

To the left and in the distance is Prior Park and the Palladian style mansion built for Ralph Allen and designed by John Wood. After making his fortune in Bath by reforming the British postal system, Allen bought the quarries on Combe Down where the golden stone-oolitic limestones – was mined to build Georgian Bath.

At North Parade Bridge, go up the steps. The top of the bridge gives the best view of the weir and Pulteney Bridge with its three arches and central Venetian window.

Reiche Kaufleute veranstalteten ihre Gesellschaftstreffen regelmäßig im prächtigen Bankettsaal des Rathauses (Foto Seite 23), das von dem Architekten Robert Adam in dem für ihn typischen Stil entworfen und 1776 eröffnet wurde.

Nebenan befindet sich der Markt, wo Sie urtümliche Spezialitäten kaufen können. Durchqueren Sie diesen Markt. Auf der Grand Parade, biegen Sie zunächst nach links ab und überqueren dann rechts die Straße, so daß Sie zur Pulteney Brücke kommen (Foto Seite 25). Diese Brücke wurde 1771 von Robert Adam gebaut, nachdem er einen Architektenwettbewerb gewonnen hatte. Sie ist die einzige Brücke in England mit Geschäften zu beiden Seiten. Lassen Ihren Blick jetzt an der Argyle Street und am Brunnen des Laura Platzes (Laura Place) vorbei zur Prachtstraße von Bath schweifen: Great Pulteney Street (Foto Seite 24)

Zu früheren Bewohnern zählten Louis Napoleon, später Napoleon III, und William Wilberforce, der die Sklaverei abschaffte. Die 330 m lange Straße wird vom 'Holburne and Menstrie Museum', das Kunstgegenstände sowie auch moderne Kunstgewerbearbeiten ausstellt, gekrönt.

Auf dem Rückweg zur Pulteney Brücke, benutzen die Treppe mit dem Hinweis: Fußweg am Fluß (Riverside Walk), der direkt am Fluß Avon zum Spazieren einlädt. Ein Marionettentheater befindet sich an der Brücke.

Laufen Sie am Wehr vorbei, bis Sie dem alten Empire Hotel praktisch gegenüberstehen. Dieses riesige Gebäude hat 3 verschiedene Dächer: das eines Schloßes, eines Herrenhauses sowie eines einfachen Hauses.

Zwischen den Hügeln können Sie in einiger Entfernung Prior Park erkennen, das Herrenhaus, das für den Steinbruchbesitzer Ralph Allen in Palladio-Stil gebaut wurde.

Wenn Sie an der North Parade Brücke (North Parade Bridge) angekommen sind, steigen Sie hier die Treppe hinauf, denn von hier bietet sich Ihnen der beste Blick auf das Wehr und die Pulteney Brücke.

Des commerçants riches tenaient leurs réunions sociales dans la magnifique salle de banquet du 'Guildhall', (photo page 23) constuite dans le style Adam et ouvert au public en 1776.

A côté, vous trouverez le marché où les passante peuvent acheter des specialités régionales comme par exemple des 'Bath Chaps' (ou joues de cochons). Traversez le marché jusqu'à 'Grand Parade', tournez à gauche et traversez la rue; vous arivez à 'Pulteney Bridge' (photo page 25) sur la droite. Ce pont fut bâti par Robert Adam en 1771 à la suite d'une compétition entre architectes. C'est le seul pont d'Angleterre possédant des magasins de chaque côté de la rue. Regardez en face de vous vers 'Argyle Street' et au-delà de la fontaine de 'Laura Place', vous verrez le Boulevard le plus imposant de Bath: 'Great Pulteney Street'. (photo page 24) Louis Napoléon, plus tard Napoléon III, et William Wilberforce, lequel abolit l'esclavage, figurent parmi ses habitants d'autrefois. A la tête de la longue rue de près de 300 mètres, se trouve le 'Holburne and Menstrie Museum' de chefs d'oeuvres et d'art moderne.

Retournez à 'Pulteney Bridge' et descendez les marches menantaux bords de la rivière Avon pour y faire une petite promenade. Un théatre de marionnettes se trouve au pied du pont.

Dépassez le barrage jusqu'à ce que vous soyez à la hauteur de l'hôtel 'Old Empire', grand bâtiment dont la silhouette exceptionelle ressemble à un château, un manoir et un cottage.

Au milieu des collines au loin, vous remarquerez 'Prior Park' et le château de style Palladio construit pour le propriétaire de la carrière de pierres, Ralph Allen.

A 'North Parade Bridge', montez les marches pour mieux voir du pont à la fois le barrage et le 'Pulteney Bridge'.

Romance is associated with the riverside grotto visible from the other side of the bridge. Here Richard Brinsley Sheridan the statesman and dramatist did his courting.

Turn right into North Parade, former home of Wordsworth the poet, Oliver Goldsmith the novelist and Edmund Burke the statesman. Here 18th century society paraded in their finery. The object was to be seen. Pierrepoint Street leading off North Parade was where Horatio Nelson, later Admiral Lord Nelson, stayed as a young captain.

To the right are the Parade Gardens *(photograph page 26)* a children's entertainment park and one of Bath's outstanding floral oases. Each year a display of succulents is planted with a theme to catch the imagination of children.

Cross Terrace Walk and head for Sally Lunn's House *(photograph page 27)* in North Parade Passage. It is the oldest house in Bath, now a refreshment house and museum. Roman remains have been found below the cellar floor indicating food was being prepared on the site 1,700 years ago. A mediaeval faggot oven, probably used to bake bread to feed workmen building the vast Norman Abbey can be seen. The present timber-framed Tudor building dates from 1482, but Sally Lunn did not arrive in Bath until 1680 to bake and hawk her brioche buns. Her shop later became a fashionable coffee house, said to be favoured by 'Beau' Nash and Ralph Allen. The secret recipe for the buns was rediscovered in a panel above the fireplace in 1966 and the buns are now sold as a delicacy.

Continue towards Abbey Green *(photograph page 28)* with its great plane tree in the centre and cross York Street to arrive back at the Abbey Churchyard.

BishopMontague

Biegen Sie jetzt zur North Parade ab, wo die Gesellschaft des 18. Jahrhunderts ihre neuesten Kreationen zur Schau trug. Auf der rechten Seite befinden sich the Parade Gärten (Parade Gardens) mit einem Park für Kinder. (Foto Seite 26) Überqueren Sie Terrace Walk und laufen Sie durch North Parade Passage zum Haus der Sally Lunn. (Foto Seite 27) Es handelt sich hierbei um das älteste Haus in Bath, das jetzt als Konditorei und Museum dient. Speisen wurden hier schon vor 1 700 Jahren zubereitet. Die berühmten 'buns', die hier noch heute zubereitet werden, stellt man nach einem uralten Geheimrezept her.

Weiter geht es über Abbey Green (Foto Seite 28) mit seiner großen, in der Mitte stehenden, Platane, nach rechts zur York Street und Sie befinden sich wieder im Abbey Churchyard.

Du pont, tournez à droite vers 'North Parade' où le beau mode faisait parade de ses richesses. A droite se trouvent les 'Parade Gardens', (photo page 26) un parc de divertissement pour les enfants.

Traversez 'Terrace Walk' et dirigez-vous vers la maison de 'Sally Lunn' (photo page 27) dans 'North Parade Passage'. C'est la plus ancienne maison de Bath qui est maintenant un salon de thé et un musée. On a cuisiné à cet emplacement il y a 1700 ans. Les célèbres petits pains que l'on sert aujourd'hui sont faits selon une ancienne recette secréte.

Continuez jusqu'à 'Abbey Green' (photo page 28) avec son grand platane au centre, et traversez 'York Street' pour vous retrouver à 'Abbey Churchyard' (ou place de l'abbaye).

Through the peaks and troughs of Bath's history, the Abbey has stood dominant for five centuries at its centre.

The site has been in continuous use for Christian worship since 676. Edgar, the first King of all England was crowned in the Saxon Abbey and all coronations since then have been based on that original ceremony.

In 1088, John de Villula was appointed Bishop of Bath and created a new cathedral so immense that the present Abbey stands within its nave. A fire in 1137 damaged the structure which was then left to decay.

A bishop's dream led to the building of the Abbey as it stands today. Bishop Oliver King, former chief secretary to King Henry VII, had a dream in which he saw angels going up and down ladders reaching to heaven. He heard voices saying "Let an olive establish the crown and a king restore the church." Bishop King interpreted this as a sign he should rebuild the Abbey. Work started in 1499.

Two master masons, Robert and William Vertue, promised him the "finest vault in England", and the Abbey's fan vaulting is its most impressive feature. The brothers built Henry VII's chapel at Westminster and William, after Robert's death, built St. George's Chapel at Windsor Castle.

Building work was stopped by Henry VIII's Dissolution of the Monasteries in 1539. Work restarted in 1574 when Elizabeth I visited Bath. Her godson Sir John Harington took her to the church during a thunderstorm and she was so shocked by the incomplete Abbey she ordered collections to be made throughout England for seven years to fund repairs.

Bishop Montague took up the restoration challenge with an enthusiastic renovation programme during his eight years as bishop between 1608-1616. Bishop Montague's brother Sir Henry donated the carved oak west doors in 1617. Bishop Montague's tomb is on the north side nave of the Abbey.

While the structure was little altered, hundreds of memorial plaques were added to the walls in the 18th and 19th centuries, including one to Richard 'Beau' Nash. Its bells rang for important visitors in Bath's Georgian heyday – or for anyone else who could afford the half a crown fee.

The Victorians added pinnacles, flying buttresses and the nave's stone fan vaulting (photograph page 30) as mason Vertue originally planned it 350 years earlier.

In 1923 the Choir Vestry was added south of the nave in memory of those who died in the 1914-18 war.

The Abbey is regarded as an outstanding example of Perpendicular English Gothic architecture, and is one of the last great churches built in this style (photograph page 29).

Viewed from Abbey Churchyard, its west front symbolically depicts Bishop Oliver King's dream of ladders reaching to heaven with falling and rising angels. Saints Peter and Paul, to whom the church is dedicated, stand on either side of the carved oak door. Over the door is a statue of Henry VII. A bishop's mitre surmounts an olive tree growing through a King's crown, to form a rebus or signature in stone.

The Abbey is called the "lantern of the west" as it features more window than wall. Most of the glass is 19th or 20th century, except the 17th century heraldic glass in the two windows in the north aisle which survived the 1942 air raids on Bath.

The city walk ends here.

Gebetet wurde an dieser Stelle schon im Jahre 676 AD. Edgar, der erste englische König, wurde hier gekrönt und seither basieren alle Krönungsfeiern auf dieser ursprünglichen Zeremonie. Die heutige 'Abbey' wurde im Jahre 1499 begonnen, einem Traum des Bischof

Oliver Kings zufolge, den er für ein Zeichen Gottes hielt. Darum wurde auf der Westseite der 'Abbey' der Traum des Bischofs mit Leitern, auf denen Engel zum Himmel hinauf – und herabsteigen, symbolisiert.

Das Fächergewölbe aus Stein im Inneren gehört zu den

eindrucksvollsten Dekorationen, (Foto Seite 30) wurde aber erst 350 Jahre nach dem ursprünglichen Entwurf fertiggestellt. Hunderte von Gedenktafeln schmücken die Wände der 'Abbey'.

Man nennt die 'Abbey' die "Laterne des Westens", da sie aus mehr Fenstern als Mauerwerk besteht. Das Glas stammt hauptsächlich aus dem 19. und 20. Jahrhundert, mit Ausnahme des heraldischen Glas in den 2 Fenstern des Nordseitenschiffs, das aus dem 17. Jahrhundert stammt und die bombenangriffe von 1942 überlebt hat.

Die 'Abbey' ist ein sehr gutes Beispiel für den englischen spätgotischen Architekturstil (Foto Seite 29).

Die Stadtführung hört hier auf, aber zu weiteren Anziehungspunkten, die sich außerhalb von Bath befinden gehören: das amerikanische Museum (American Museum) in der Claverton Manor, das (Bath Industrial Heritage Centre) und Beckfords Turm (Beckford's Tower) am Lansdown.

Innerhalb einer Stunde können Bristol und Wells, die Cheddarschlucht (Cheddar Gorge), die Herrenhäuser Dyrham Park und Longleat, die Stourhead Gärten (Stourhead Gardens) und die Dörfer Castle Combe und Lacock erreicht werden.

C'est un cité religieux depuis 676 ap. J.C. Edgar, premier Roi d'Angleterre fut couronné ici et les couronnements à partir de cette époque ont été basés sur la cérémonie originelle.

Cette abbaye date de 1499 et fut bâtit à la suite d'un rêve que fit le Bishop Oliver King, qu'il traduit comme étant un signe de Dieu. La façade Ouest de l'Abbaye dépeint symboliquement le rêve de Bishop Oliver King avec ses échelies montant vers le paradis, et ses anges montants et tombants.

La plus impressionnante particularité de l'Abbaye est ses voûtes en éventail, en pierres, (photo page 30) mais celles-ci ne furent achevées que 350 après leur conception originelle. Des centaines de plaques commémoratives couvrent les murs de l'Abbaye.

On appelle l'Abbaye la 'lanterne de l'ouest' car elle possède plus de vitraux que de murs. La plupart des vitraux datent du 19 et 20 ième siècle à part les vitraux héraldiques du 17 ième siècle des 2 fenêtres de la nef latérale nord, qui ont survécu aux bombardements aériens de Bath en 1942. L'Abbaye est un exemple saillant du style d'architecture Gothique Anglais Perpendiculaire. (photo page 29)

L'excursion se termine ici, mais vous trouverez d'autres attractions en dehors de Bath, comme le 'American Museum' (ou musée americain) à 'Claverton Manor', et le Bath Industrial Heritage Centre, puis la 'Beckford's Tower' à Lansdown.

A une heure d'ici en voiture, vous pouvez visiter les villes de Bristol et de Wells; Cheddar Gorge, les châteaux de 'Dyrham Park' et de 'Longleat', 'Stourhead Gardens' et les villages de 'Castle Combe' et 'Lacock'.

Further attractions can be found in Bath's outskirts.

Three miles from the city is the American Museum at Claverton Manor. It shows domestic life in America from the late 17th to 19th centuries, and the work of American craftsmen.

At Prior Park College, the former home of Ralph Allen, the chapel and part of the grounds are open to the public. It is the finest and grandest Palladian style mansion in Britain.

The Bath Industrial Heritage Centre, Morford Street in Lansdown recreates an engineering works at the turn of the century and tells the story of Bath stone. Beckford's Tower, built in 1827 on Lansdown Hill gives extensive views over the city.

Within an hour's drive are the cities of Bristol and Wells; Cheddar Gorge and stately homes including Dyrham Park and Longleat; Stourhead Gardens and the villages of Castle Combe and Lacock and the ancient monuments of Stonehenge and Avebury.

The Ironmonger's Shop, Bath Industrial Heritage Centre

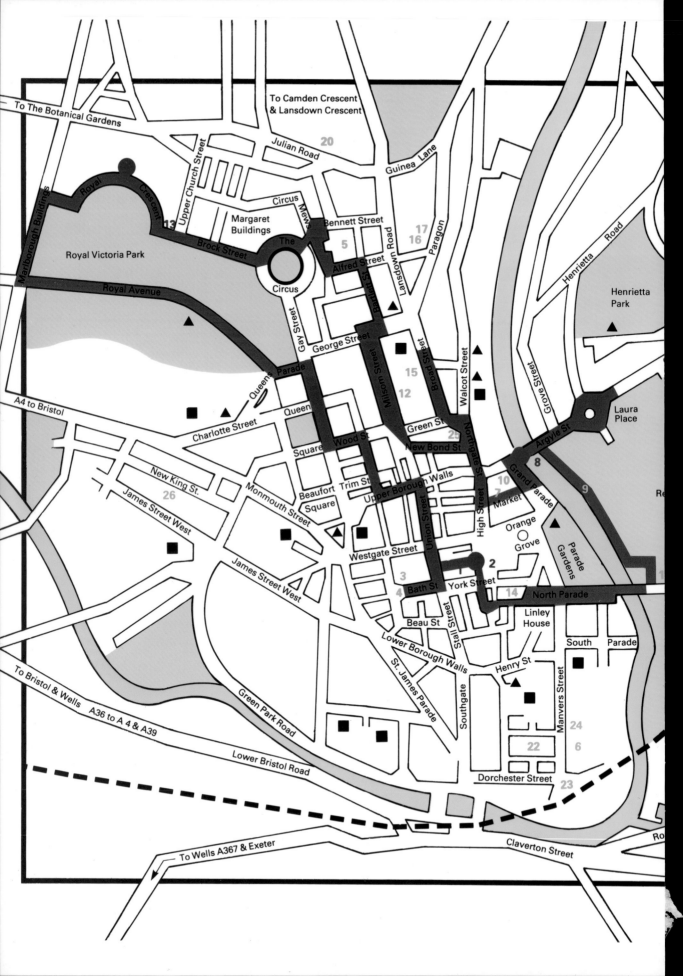